DEVELOPING YOUR CHILD'S SELF-WORTH

KAY KUZMA

Pacific Press® Publishing Association
Nampa, Idaho
Oshawa, Ontario, Canada

Edited by Marvin Moore
Designed by Linda Griffith
Cover photo by Betty Blue
Type set in 10/12 Century Schoolbook

ISBN 0-8163-0833-0

98 99 00 01 ● 9 8 7

Developing Your Child's Self-Worth

You could tell Jamie didn't feel good about himself just by looking at him: sad, downcast eyes, slumped shoulders, and shuffling feet. He was a good-looking lad, but he constantly downgraded himself, picking out personal faults that were not obvious to others, such as his slightly crooked teeth. In school Jamie was a loner; he spoke only when he was spoken to and then in such a low voice that it was difficult to hear his response. He had many talents, such as drawing and athletic skills, but when asked to exhibit his artwork or take part in varsity, he just shrugged his shoulders and declined.

How your child feels about himself or herself is the single greatest factor in determining future happiness and well-being. Does he see himself as someone of high value, or as someone worthless? Does she realistically accept her abilities and limitations, or does she feel inadequate and often wish she were someone else?

Your child may have beauty and brains, riches and talent, and your family may be well-known and highly respected, but if your child dislikes himself and feels inferior, these assets will be of little benefit.

Sometimes the signs of low self-worth can be seen clearly, like with Jamie. On the other hand, they may be masked by what appears to be a superiority complex.

From the time Cheri was a little girl, she clamored to be the center of attention. She bragged, showed off, fabricated stories to make herself look better, tattled on others, and constantly talked about herself. Most people never guessed that Cheri was suffering from a low self-concept. Acting superior was her way of overcoming these negative feelings about herself and of gaining the recognition she craved.

Feelings of low self-worth may be so hidden that parents are unaware of their child's internal struggle.

To all outside appearances, Sarah should have felt on top of the world. A teenager, she had everything going for her. Her teachers loved her, her peers admired her, she was a student leader, and she was active in her church. Her parents prided themselves on having the "perfect" daughter, because she never gave them a moment's worry. They recognized her faults, of course, like spending too much money when she went shopping and procrastinating about her homework, but these were minor, and her parents were sure these would fade away with maturity.

But Sarah didn't feel good about herself. She was beautiful—but never quite as pretty as some other girl. She maintained a 3.9 grade-point average—but someone always got better grades. Sarah had an internal need for perfection that she could never quite live up to. She felt like a failure and suffered from feelings of low self-worth. Sarah's faults were not a maturity problem, as her parents thought, but symptoms of her self-worth problem: spending money to always have the best, and missing homework deadlines because she was trying to do a perfect job.

Developing self-worth is a complex task. There is no magic formula, no simple answer. Every child, no matter how capable, will at times suffer from feelings of inferiority and failure. But you, Mom and Dad, can be a significant factor in helping your child feel valuable, regardless of the circumstances he or she encounters. With the proper preparation, you can be aware of the subtle signs of low self-worth from which your child suffers. You can then map out a plan to help your child through the difficult times in his life so that he grows up to be a happy, healthy person who feels valuable because of who he is—and because of what God has done for him.

Your goal, then, is to help your child develop into a functioning, happy, competent individual—someone with a healthy sense of self-worth. You can do this if you understand how your words and actions affect your child's feelings and how he or she develops a positive self-concept.

Help Your Child to Feel Valuable

Self-esteem begins with the feeling that "I'm worth something," not only to myself, but to others. The challenge for parents is to help their children feel valuable.

Two things combine to help a child feel valuable: desirability and competence. Desirability means that your child feels wanted. Competence means that he feels useful and productive. You can build your child's feelings of desirability and competence by kind words, positive expectations, and considerate behavior. On the other hand, thoughtless words, negative expectations, and harsh behavior quickly destroy her self-worth.

As you read the following sections, ask yourself whether the words, expectations, and behavior your child receives from you are usually positive, or whether they tend to be more negative.

Words that make or break self-worth

You've probably heard the old saying, "Sticks and stones can break my bones, but words can never hurt me."

Don't believe it! Thoughtless words *can* hurt. They can destroy.

Monitor your words carefully, paying special attention to the tone of voice with which you say them. A good rule is to always speak the way you would like others to speak to you. Listen to yourself talk to your child. If what you hear would upset you if your spouse or a friend spoke to you that way, think of a better way to get your message across to your child.

In the following examples, the negative way is mentioned first to help you understand why the positive way is better. As you read each statement, ask yourself whether it makes you feel wanted or unwanted, competent or incompetent. You can be sure your child feels the same way.

Negative: "Why did you do that?"
Positive: "Tell me how you feel."

Negative: "Can't you ever do anything right?"
Positive: "Can you think of a better way to do that?"

Negative: "You're driving me crazy!"
Positive: "What would you like to do today?"

Negative: "Why don't you leave me alone?"
Positive: "I'm busy right now, but as soon as I've finished, I'll help you."

Negative: "You deserve what you got!"

Positive: "If this happens again, what could you do so no one gets hurt?"

Negative: "You know better than that."
Positive: "Remember the rule next time."

Expectations that make or break self-worth

I knew a mother once who was always apologizing to her friends for her children's misbehavior. "Julie's such a destructive child," she would say, or, "Michael's always getting into things that don't belong to him."

Guess what? Julie and Michael did indeed destroy things at times, and they were always getting into things that didn't belong to them. Children tend to fulfill the expectations they hear. If you *expect* your child to misbehave, he probably will. On the other hand, if you always express confidence in her behavior when you're with friends—even when you don't feel confident—she will be much more likely to act that way.

Parents, remember that *you write the script for your child's behavior.*

Here's a little self-test. Compare the following casual comments with the things you say about your children when you're with friends. If you can "hear" yourself saying too many of them, the evaluation that follows may help you to be more positive in the expectations you express.

"He always resists."
"She never cleans her room."
"He's a liar."
"She's a showoff."
"He's never on time."
"She's a klutz—always knocking things over."

9

What's wrong with these statements? First, they focus on a negative aspect of the child's behavior. No one likes to have others call attention to their faults.

Second, they label the child—calling him a liar, a showoff, a klutz.

And third, they use the words *always* and *never*, as though your child has no positive traits and will never change.

To help your child feel valuable, avoid saying anything negative about him unless you can precede or follow the comment with something positive. Here are some examples, with the positive part italicized:

Negative: "He always resists."
Positive: *"He's usually a pretty compliant kid,* but things aren't going so well today. We have a little resistance."

Negative: "She never cleans her room."
Positive: "It's not easy keeping a room clean, but *she's getting better at it."*

Negative: "He's a liar!"
Positive: *"He has quite an imagination.* What he said just now probably didn't happen quite that way."

At other times, you can simply say what you need to say in a less condemning way, like this:

Negative: "She's a showoff."
Positive: "She enjoys getting attention."

Negative: "He's always late."

Positive: "Being on time is not very important to him."

Do you see the difference? Neither of these positive statements will be as likely to destroy your child's self-worth. Please notice, however, that both of them suggest an expectation that you may not want your child to imitate. The best way is to excuse the misbehavior gently while stating the positive behavior you expect, as in the three preceding examples.

When you need to correct your child, state the facts rather than assassinating character. Notice the difference between these two statements:

Negative: "You're a klutz! You're always knocking things over!"

Positive: "It's sometimes difficult for you to control your movements. You have to be extra careful around things that can get knocked over."

Which statement would you rather someone made to you? Obviously, the second! The first attacks the child's character. The second focuses on a fact.

Behavior that makes or breaks self-worth

Pretend that you are a helpless baby in the crib, and you're hungry and cold. Your bottom stings because of your messy diaper, and your neck is getting stiff from lying in the same position so long. What would you do? Cry, of course! You have no idea it's the middle of the night. All you know is that you're miserable.

Suppose your mother let's you cry for an hour, and when she does come she yanks you out of the crib, shakes you, curses you in a harsh tone, and then slams you back into the crib and shoves a bottle of cold water into your mouth. How would you feel?

It's experiences like this one, repeated over and over, that cause a child to grow up feeling worthless. He reasons that if he were worth something, he would be treated better.

Most children have loving parents who wouldn't think of treating them with such thoughtless neglect or cruelty. But these same loving parents do get frustrated at times, and on occasion lash out verbally, and sometimes physically, at their children.

Don't take your frustrations out on your child! It only causes her to feel worthless. Take a break when you're close to exploding. Ask someone else to watch your child for a while, or call someone who can give you a word of encouragement.

Signs of Low Self-Worth

Low self-worth does not develop suddenly. It's a slow process that evolves as a child perceives that the significant people in his life don't think very much of him. In reality, they may love and care for him very much, but his *perception* is the important factor. If a child feels that his own parents don't love him or don't think that he is as good as other children, his belief in himself will be seriously damaged. Even if his parents shower him with love and support, there may be periods when he feels that other people don't like him or that his friends reject him. When this occurs, his self-concept may suffer.

The visible signs of low self-esteem are related to a child's age. For example, excessive thumb sucking might be considered a sign of low self-worth for a seven- or eight-year-old, but could be very normal for a one- or two-year-old. These signs are also situation related. For example, a certain behavior may occur when the child is with strangers or when he is very tired—an indication that he feels insecure only in certain situations or under certain circumstances.

The next section mentions a number of behaviors that are characteristic of preschool and school-age children with low self-esteem. Don't immediately assume that your child has an emotional problem because he or she exhibits some of these signs. Consider such behavior an indication that you need to spend a little more time with her to convince her that she is a worthwhile person. This is a good time to formulate a plan to help her feel more desirable and competent.

If your child exhibits quite a few of the following behaviors, you may want to seek professional help to find out the cause of his negative feelings toward himself. The earlier you assess your child's self-worth problem and the earlier you seek help, the easier it will be to get him back on the road to developing a healthy self-concept.

After each characteristic of low self-worth mentioned below are several suggestions for bolstering your child's ego and helping him to realize his true value. These suggestions should be a helpful guide throughout childhood, but will be particularly meaningful during the early years.

Unrealistic fears

Fear of games. Some children are afraid to play games, especially competitive games. If this is your child's problem, try playing noncompetitive games. Give a prize for *playing* rather than for *winning*. Spend time teaching your child the skills and strategies that he needs in order to win part of the time.

13

Fear of questions. It is hard for some children to ask questions. Others have a hard time answering. Make it easy for your child to ask questions. Say something like, "It looks as if you have a good question for me." Encourage questions when you are alone with him or in a safe family setting. Reward her for asking questions with responses like, "That's a good question," or, "I can tell you are really thinking," when she does ask.

Also, ask your child questions. Make them simple at first, with obvious answers, and accept all answers by saying something like, "That's an interesting idea."

Saying, "I don't know how." All of us experience times when we really don't know how to do something. Suspect a low self-worth problem, though, if you hear your child say this quite often. Reassure him that it is OK not to know how. Say, "When I was your age, I didn't know either." Offer to do it yourself, and "hire" him as your special assistant. Let him do any small part of the task that he is obviously capable of doing.

Afraid to try. Sometimes children are afraid to try something new, even when an adult offers to help. A good way to handle this is to let the child watch a new activity before encouraging him to try it. Let him decide when he will try. If he has a hard time deciding, say, "How long do you think you'll want to watch before trying?" After he indicates the amount of time he needs, tell him to let you know when he's ready so you can help him.

Fear of new situations or people. Some children shrink at being left in new situations with strange people. If your child has this problem, stay with him until he feels comfortable. Ask him to tell you when it is OK for you to leave. Don't appear anxious to go. After a reasonable time, warn him, "I will have to leave in ten minutes." When the time is up, go to your child, say "goodbye," and tell him or her when you will

14

return. Then leave, and keep your promise by returning on time.

Unusual or negative behavior

Crying, pouting to get own way. We've all seen children who cried, pouted, or threw themselves on the floor to get their own way. We call it a "tantrum." Ignore the behavior, but acknowledge the feelings. Say things like, "I can tell it makes you sad when you don't get what you want. I sometimes feel that way too." Then give your child something positive to do, like bouncing a ball. Or say, "This is what I do when I feel that way (name an activity). What are some other things you could do to chase away the sad feelings?"

Carries a blanket or pacifier, sucks thumb. Some children's unusual behavior results from a need for security. Two common examples are attachment to an object such as a blanket, and sucking, usually on a thumb or pacifier. A good way to handle this is to give your child extra attention, without letting him know that his behavior bothers you. Keep her busy. A three-year-old child can make up his or her mind to give up the pacifier or blanket. Let him buy something he really wants in exchange for it. Let him actually give it away to the store clerk! Just be sure that it's the child's decision, not yours that is urged on him.

Biting, kicking, hitting, spitting. What can you do about a child who bites, kicks, hits, or spits? As long as nobody's getting hurt, one good way is to ignore the negative behavior and reward positive behavior. These actions indicate that your child is discouraged and unhappy, so encourage him. Find the little things he does well and capitalize on them. Stop behavior that is threatening to others by saying, "I can't let you hurt someone else," but don't belittle your child with criticism.

Misbehaving and disturbing others. Some children are showoffs, while others seem to enjoy pushing themselves around and getting in the way. Some will deliberately do the very thing they are asked not to do. These are attention-getting devices. If you catch the misbehavior before it has gotten to the point of requiring discipline, just give the child the attention she needs. Try saying, "I'll bet you'd like me to play with you. Let's go . . . " Try inventing a special word that you'll both understand—perhaps a secret word that nobody else knows—so that your child can use the word when he desperately needs attention and won't have to resort to inappropriate behavior to get it. Then be sure you always respond to that word!

Excessive concern about acceptance

Giving things away. Occasionally I see a child with a compulsive urge to give her things away. She's really trying to buy acceptance. Concentrate on showing her how much you like her because she exists. Compliment your child on things she or he can't change: blue eyes, black curly hair, etc. Spend time with him that is not related to receiving a gift. Explain that the most important gift is friendship because it can't be broken or lost. Encourage your child to invite a friend home to play. Help him make friends without giving gifts.

Giving to teacher. A special form of the "giving away" syndrome is the constant desire to give things to the teacher or to friends at school. If this is your child's problem, make it a policy that he can only take things to school for "show and tell" sessions (other than books, notebooks, pencils, etc.). Let the teacher know why you think your child is doing this, and work together to meet his need for attention and approval.

Asks, "Do you love me?" Take it as a possible sign of insecurity if your child constantly asks you or others, "Do you like me?" or, "Do you love me?" I recommend that you read Mariam Schlein's picture book *The Way Mothers Are* to your child each day for a month, and let your behavior give the same unconditional "I love you" message.

Exaggeration and unrealistic expectations

"They don't like me." Did your child ever come running home, tears all over his face, crying, "They don't like me! They don't like me!"? That's normal—up to a point. When it gets to be an obsession, suspect a self-esteem problem. Don't disagree by saying, "Sure they do," or, "That's not true." Instead, try saying, "You must really feel hurt. Tell me more." Encourage him or her to think of ways to change the situation.

Bragging and boasting. On the other side of the spectrum are children who appear overly confident. They continually brag and boast. Often, of course, they are compensating for a much deeper insecurity. Try shocking your child by agreeing with him. "Yes, you are an important person, and you *can* do a lot of things better than (the other person). Let's talk about the things you can do better." Think of obvious things (if the child is smaller, he can crawl through a much smaller hole). However, put things in perspective also. Mention that everyone can do something better than others, and that there is always someone who can do some things better than he can. Ask your child to help you think of some of those things too.

Jealousy. Take it as a possible sign of low self-esteem when a child shows excessive jealousy over the attention others receive from teachers and friends. The best way to handle this is to see that your child receives lots of your attention. Arrange, also, for others to spend time with him or her. Invite friends his or her own age over to play. In-

17

vite the child's teacher to your home for supper some evening, with a special "bug in her ear" to give lots of attention to the child. Usually, when the child's need for love and attention is met, he will not feel jealous.

Perfectionism. Some children show extreme concern over not being perfect. They'll tear up art work that isn't just so, or they're afraid of going to school because they won't know a spelling word. Some children get very depressed if they don't make 100 percent or an A on every paper. This is an early sign of perfectionism. Be especially careful not to add to their distress by expressing high expectations. These children need unconditional acceptance regardless of their performance, especially when they feel like a failure. Encourage your child to talk about his feelings of wanting everything perfect; then turn the conversation to the value of trying regardless of the quality of the performance. Explain how much we learn through mistakes.

Difficulty with social relationships

Extreme competitiveness. Some children have a particularly hard time learning to be a good sport. Often this is a clue to an inner insecurity. While you don't want to ignore it when your child wins, avoid making a long-term affair out of it. Put trophies in the child's room rather than the front room, and avoid lauding your child in front of relatives and friends. When the child loses, let him know that you accept him whether he wins or loses.

Avoids defending herself. The opposite of the child who is a bully is the one who refuses to stand up for his or her own rights at all. If this is your child's problem, encourage her to stand up for her rights by saying, "You are an important person. Don't allow others to hurt you needlessly." Then give her the words to use in future situations, such as, "You may not say those things to me." Role-play with the child the words and tone of voice to use.

Is critical and judgmental. A critical spirit that is encouraged—even allowed—in childhood can ruin an adult's life. Tattling falls into the same category. It is often a sign of insecurity and low self-worth. Do not accept tattling, and do not reward it. Change the topic of conversation, and give your best attention when the child is not tattling or criticizing.

Components of Self-Worth

A healthy self-concept is made up of five important factors:

1. **Self-image**: How he views his appearance
2. **Self-esteem**: How he feels he is regarded by others
3. **Self-confidence**: How competent he feels about his skills and abilities
4. **Self-respect**: How he feels when he does what he knows is right and honorable
5. **Value to God**: Accepting himself because of the value God sees in him

Because these five components are so important to self-worth, the next few sections will focus on how you can develop them in your child's life.

Self-image

Your child's self-image is how he thinks he looks. Feelings about self-image are not always stable. Children often compare their looks to others and feel that they are not as attractive. A child may feel good about how he looks when he is with one group, but in another group with different hairstyles, clothing, and behavior, the same child may feel dreadfully inferior.

It's very difficult to think positively of others when you feel miserable about yourself. For example, if you are dressed inappropriately for a party, who do you think about all evening? Children who feel good about their appearance will find it easier to forget about themselves and focus on others.

However, helping a child to feel good about his or her appearance may not be easy. Do you sometimes feel like tearing your hair out when you see your child's hairstyle? You may feel frustrated putting up with current styles, but for your child's sake it is very important that you grin and bear it. Remember that this too shall pass!

Acceptable appearance is culturally determined. What is acceptable to you may not be acceptable to your child. Watching the kids on a high school campus is almost like watching a costume party. It's difficult for me to understand why kids stand in front of the mirror for three hours every morning working on how sloppy they can make their hair and clothes look!

In the 1980s flat top hair styles for boys were "in." Unfortunately, instead of flat tops with the duck tails of the fifties, which I thought looked quite stylish, these kids let a long bleached portion of hair fall down into their eyes! And they don't wear socks. All winter—no socks. Crazy! What ever happened to nice jackets? These kids wear boxy jackets with sleeves pushed up to the elbows that look like they have slept in them. And their pants—baggy! And rolled up tight at the bottom. Just a few years before, if I'd suggested to my son Kevin that he roll up his pants, he'd have fainted in embarrassment.

And the girls' appearance is just as bad. Can you

imagine getting a permanent and then not curling your frizzy hair? And if it doesn't stick out enough, just mousse and "Spritz-Forte" it! When I was a teenager we went through agony, sleeping on those big, hard, prickly rollers just to make sure no one ever saw us looking like that! That dates me, doesn't it?

And as for a girl's clothing, it's tight pants, shirts with long tails hanging—and sweaters above the tails! Or sweaters hanging down around the knees. Most parents agree that their kids look awful, but that's according to our perception of what is proper dress—not theirs.

Why do kids work so hard to look the way they do? Because their self-worth depends on it! Self-image—how they look to themselves—is a vital part of their self-concept, and to preserve a healthy self-concept, they've got to wear hairdos and clothing that are accepted by their culture, regardless of what adults consider to be good taste.

When a kid thinks he looks right, he feels good about himself. He tends to smile more often and feel more comfortable with friends. He can forget about his looks and concentrate on others. But if he perceives he's dressed all wrong, he can't think anything but self-condemning thoughts.

So if you want your child to feel good about himself, you've got to recognize that his looks must be acceptable to his peers. Remember that the better he feels about his appearance, the more likely he will have the inner strength to say No to really important things like drugs, alcohol, and tobacco. On the other hand, the worse he feels about his appearance, the more likely he will conform to negative peer pressure in order to gain a measure of acceptance.

Here are some things you can do to help your child feel good about his appearance.

Physical defects. Not every child is born perfect. In fact, most kids at some time during their growing years wish their genes and chromosomes had made them better looking.

You can help your child to feel good about his physical characteristics by complimenting him on things he can't easily change: "I love that sparkle in your eyes." "Your smile is a winner." "You've got the cutest dimples—I always wished I had dimples." "You're so lucky to have naturally curly hair—it's my favorite."

Some children have the misfortune to be born with obvious physical defects: A birth mark, ears that stick out, knock-knees, buck teeth that take years of braces to straighten. Major defects include being born with no hand or with one leg shorter than the other or with a hearing or visual handicap or with a disease such as cerebral palsy. These children must accept their bodies. To do this, it is extremely important that you can accept them first. Don't treat their appearance as a handicap. Instead, do everything possible to help them overcome what may be considered a negative. For example, get braces for the child who hates to smile because of crooked teeth. Teach a deaf child to read lips so he can interact more easily with friends who can hear.

Hair and dress styles. Every child's appearance can be enhanced by dressing in colors that complement skin tones, hair, and eye color. This is especially true for girls. Hairstyles can do a lot to bring out the attractive features of a child's face. Many physical "defects" can be camouflaged by dress styles. For example, diagonal stripes are more complimentary to the plump child than horizontal stripes. With the proper training, children can learn to hide many of their physical blemishes, making their appearance more pleasing.

Principles of appearance. It isn't necessary to wear

outlandish clothing, flashy jewelry, gaudy makeup, and bizarre hairstyles to be acceptable to peers. Establish the basic principles of appearance during the early years: principles such as modesty, simplicity, and durability, that can guide your child in making appropriate clothing selections. There is a wide variety of acceptable and trendy fashions that don't violate these basic principles.

Remember, it's not how *you* think your child looks that affects his self-concept. It's how *he* thinks he looks. So, depending upon the fashion of the day, you may have to swallow your own bias. Instead of trying to make your child look right in *your* sight, make sure he looks right in *his* sight, and you'll help him to develop a positive self-image. Then he won't have to constantly think about his own looks, but can focus his attention on others.

Self-esteem

Self-esteem is how valuable you feel, based upon how you perceive others feel about you. It's like a mirror. You see yourself through the eyes of others.

Have you ever been at the top of the roller coaster track and experienced the excitement of the ride to come? Ahhh! It's fun to be at the top. And having a positive feeling about yourself is like being at the top of the roller coaster with all its feelings of anticipation and excitement. Unfortunately, we too often find ourselves at the bottom! Because it depends upon what we perceive others feel about us, self-esteem is an up-and-down experience. With one person we feel great; with another, lousy. For a better idea of how this works, let's observe Joyce.

Joyce is a lovely girl—not as outgoing as some, but a lot of fun to be with when you get to know her. She gets good grades and has musical talent. She comes from a good, stable family who love her dearly and think she's special. Joyce has a lot going for her. And, generally, she feels pretty good about herself.

But Joyce is a little unsure of herself in social situations. She is only a sophomore, but she has her eyes on a good-looking senior who is captain of the football team. She wants to ask him to the reverse banquet and has been practicing just how to do it. She'll walk up to his locker between second and third period, smile, and say . . .

She finally decides that today is the day! Her friends encourage her. She has just walked across campus with Nelson, the kid she's grown up with. He thinks Joyce is pretty special, and Joyce knows how he feels. They tease each other and laugh. She feels good about herself. In fact, she feels wonderful. She's at the top of the roller coaster!

There's still five minutes before the bell rings for third period. She has time. Suddenly, there's Joe, the football captain, getting something out of his locker. She takes a deep breath, smiles, and confidently walks up to him. "Hi, Joe," she says with a lilt in her voice. Joe totally ignores her, continuing instead to look for something in his locker. She musters up her courage again. "Hi, Joe, there's something I've been wanting to ask you."

Joe slams his locker shut and mutters "Ya?" as he spots the campus beauty queen and yells to her, "Wait up, Sheila. I'll walk with you." He dashes off after Sheila without a second look at Joyce.

Joyce feels angry, hurt, and depressed. Her smile fades, and she wants to crawl into a hole. She's a social failure. She's nothing. She's at the bottom of the roller coaster, and life at this moment isn't worth living.

Self-esteem is a very shaky thing. It all depends on how you perceive the people in your life feel about you. One minute you're up—if you're with someone like Nelson who you know thinks you're terrific. The next minute you're down—if you bump into a Joe, who ignores you and brushes you off for someone else.

How can you help your child "keep up" in the area of self-esteem?

First, reflect your feeling that he's OK. Be sure your child sees in your words and actions the message that he is special. You never know when your kid will bump into someone who sends her to the bottom of the roller coaster. It sure helps a kid to get back up to the top when she knows, without a shadow of a doubt, that she's "A one" in her parents' eyes!

Help your child understand the roller-coaster effect of self-esteem. He can be up one minute because someone complimented him, and down the next because someone was critical. He's the same person. His feelings about himself changed because of the way he was treated.

It's impossible to keep a child from bumping into people who treat him negatively. By showing your child that *you* think he's special, he will be better able to get through those hurtful times and maintain a positive self-concept.

Self-confidence

Self-confidence is the ability to step out into the world and meet various situations without falling apart! The more skills and abilities a child develops in different areas, the more resources he will have to meet new situations in life.

The child who is skilled in one area develops confidence that he can succeed in other areas. Your child may never have taken chemistry, but because he got A's in physics, he can walk confidently into chemistry, ready to tackle the elements!

Mary was not a brilliant child. She seemed shy and reserved—afraid to try new things. She lacked confidence. So her father planned a program to help Mary build skills and abilities in a wide variety of areas that would ultimately help her feel more confident.

Academic skills are especially important, so he started there. He believed that kids who are exposed to various subjects in the safety of their home have more confidence when they hit the classroom. Before Mary even started school, Dad had her working on math concepts a year or two ahead of first grade. He avoided overteaching so that she'd "forget" certain concepts. That way she was not bored in school, yet when the teacher explained something it immediately sounded familiar to her, and she quickly grasped the concept. This boosted her self-confidence tremendously.

Dad also felt that the ability to speak a foreign language was a foundation skill every child should learn, so during those early childhood years he hired a French tutor. High-school French was a breeze for Mary, and when she later decided to go to graduate school, she had no trouble with the foreign language requirement.

Work was also important, especially useful work that built practical skills. The family bought land in apple-growing country and lived in a trailer for three years while they built their own home. They planted an orchard together, and the kids learned about grafting, pruning, fertilizing, and everything else that goes into taking care of trees. They also learned to press juice, and sold their produce at their own fruit stand.

Taking care of horses, skunks, raccoons, and dogs, plus piano lessons rounded out Mary's home training.

What effect did all this have on Mary? After graduating from college, she set her sites on Stanford University and began preparing for the qualifying exams. Because vocabulary was her weakest area, she learned the definition of every word ever to appear on the test and scored in the highest percentile! She's completing a post-doctoral research fellowship, is married, has a two-year-old and another on the way, and continues to look forward to life with confidence.

The wide variety of experiences she had during childhood gave her the skills she needed to tackle the world with confidence.

Each new skill or ability that your child develops will contribute to his or her feelings of confidence. Search for your child's unique talents. What about tinkering with an old car or playing a harmonica? Maybe it's something you can do together, such as playing tennis or putting together a remote-control vehicle. Help your child develop the skills and abilities he needs to face the future with confidence.

Self-respect

A child respects himself when he does what he knows he should do. Encourage your child to value honesty, integrity, and dependability; to stick up for the rights of others; and to speak out against injustice! Teach your child that he should not demean himself by ignoring his conscience—his self-respect is too important.

Does your child realize that every time he yields to temptation, whether it's taking that extra piece of pie or screaming at Mom and Dad, he is chipping away at his self-respect—the fourth vital component of a healthy self-concept?

Although he might not be able to do much about his self-image, self-esteem, and self-confidence, he can control his feelings of self-respect by doing what he knows he ought to do.

That's not as easy as it sounds. When I lecture on the subject of self-concept, and especially the importance of self-respect, I often challenge my listeners by asking, "How many of you have ever gone through a long checkout line at the supermarket, and then discovered when

27

you got in the car that the clerk forgot to charge you for a certain item?" This has probably happened to all of us. What do you do? Chances are you begin rationalizing, "Well, I shop here all the time, and I didn't use those double-discount coupons last week, and a couple of months ago they overcharged me on an item that was supposed to be discounted, so I guess that makes us about even." If that's what you do, you are tearing down your self-concept. Your self-respect drops when you don't do what you know you should.

This happened to me one day. I was in a hurry, but decided to stop by my favorite discount mart to see what sales they had in the nursery department. I loaded my cart with plants, and on the way to the checkout stand I picked up a thirty-nine-cent package of swiss chard seeds. The clerk counted up my plants without removing them from the cart, and I completely forgot about that little thirty-nine-cent package of seeds until I was loading the plants into the car. There it was, still in the cart. "Oh, no," I sighed, "I bet she forgot to charge me for this." I checked the sales receipt, and, sure enough, there was no thirty-nine cents.

"Now, what should I do?" I thought. "I'm already in a hurry. Do I go back and stand in line to pay for these seeds, or should I just forget about it? After all, I do so much shopping in this store that from the money they have made off me, they can afford to give me the seeds."

I was really tempted to do just that. In fact, had I not used that illustration in my lectures, I might have yielded. But I thought, "How can I do this when I advise others not to tear down their self-respect by doing things they know they shouldn't?" So back to the check-out stand I marched. I waited for the checker to finish with a customer, and then I broke line. "I'm sorry," I said, "but this package of seeds was hidden under my plants, and you forgot to charge me for it," and I handed the clerk the money.

You should have seen the expression on that clerk's face—and on the faces of the other people in line. Shock! Total shock, that someone had actually come back to pay for a thirty-nine-cent mistake. One of the people in line even commented, "Boy, I really admire you for that." The clerk thanked me again and again.

How do you think I felt as I left that store? Ten feet tall! I can't remember ever doing anything that made me feel more valuable.

So when everything else seems to be going wrong for your child, and his sense of value is slipping, encourage him to listen carefully to his conscience and keep doing what he knows is right—because self-respect is a *very* important part of his self-concept.

God's value

When life seems to be battering your child's self-image, her self-esteem, her confidence and self-respect, it's time to remind her that she can preserve her self-concept by realizing how much God values her. Teach your child that God created her a unique and special human being (see Psalm 139:13-16), and that God loves her so much that He sent His Son to die for her (see John 3:16). Best of all, God has a restoration plan for her (see John 14:1-3). Tell your child that God wouldn't go to all this trouble if she weren't valuable! Never let her forget that!

Christians have a wonderful advantage when it comes to *really* feeling valuable, having that true sense of self-worth.

The world tells us we are valuable, and that regardless of our feelings, we just have to believe it to be a fact. Humanistic theory says a person can pull himself up by his own bootstraps. There are encounter groups, therapy sessions, weekend serendipity workshops, and all types of professionals trying new techniques and theories to make people believe that they are valuable.

All of these ideas are important, but they don't offer the best answer! What should a child do when, no matter how she tries to pull herself up by her own bootstraps, she just keeps tripping? She's gone to a color analyst, lost fifteen pounds, and restyled her hair—and she still doesn't look like Marilyn Monroe. Her self-image still has flaws.

You have taught her to carefully choose her friends, making sure she's around positive people who like her. She tries to avoid critical and sarcastic comments in order to keep her self-esteem as high as possible, but still there are times when she feels rejected.

You have stressed how important self-confidence is to the total feeling of self, and you've encouraged her to take a computer course so she can interact intelligently with her computer friends who speak computerese. She's even increased her typing speed in order to compete for a good summer job. But no matter how many new skills she develops, she still quakes anytime she is asked to do something new.

And, as hard as she tries, she still yields to temptations—like eating that double fudge sundae or staying out past her curfew. And there goes her self-respect! How can she feel valuable when nothing seems to be going right in her life?

This is where Christianity parts company from the humanistic philosophy of existence. This is where Christianity holds the trump card. Christianity deals with a person's true worth, his real value. Of all the lessons of life that you must teach your child, the most important is that God values him no matter what! By believing that God made him, your child can feel valuable even when everything around him seems to be in shambles. God created him, and there is not one other person in this entire universe that is exactly like him. Your child is special, known by God from the moment of his conception. That's a powerful fact to strengthen one's self-worth!

But added to this, God died for your child. She has sinned and because of that, she has been condemned to die. But God said, "No! I will die for you." And He did. God the Son died at the hands of wicked, torturing men—so that your child could live. She is so valuable that God gave His Son's life for her, and He would have done it even if she had been the only person in the universe to have sinned.

Because God made your child and died for him, he has a right to feel so valuable that nothing could ever again demean him. And there's more. Not only did God make each person special and die for each, He also has a plan for each one. He has a work for your child to do for Him that no one else can do, and when that work is done, He plans for your child to live with Him throughout eternity. What a gift!

Mom, Dad, don't ever let your children forget who they really are—and the value God places in them. That's true self-worth!

For further reading:

Briggs, Dorothy Corkille. *Your Child's Self-Esteem*. Garden City, N.Y.: Doubleday & Company, Inc., 1967.

Dobson, James. *Hide or Seek*. Old Tappan, N.Y.: Fleming H. Revell Company, 1974.

Kuzma, Kay. *To Understand Your Child*. Box 2222, Redlands, Calif.: Family Matters, Inc., 1985.

Is your child shy around strangers? Does he bully the children at school? Odd as it may seem, both of these behaviors are signs of low self-esteem. If you've suffered from low self-esteem, you know how hard it is to overcome the problem once you're an adult.

In this book Kay Kuzma outlines the basic elements of self-esteem and explains how you can develop these in your children while they are still young and impressionable. She explains the symptoms of low self-esteem in children so that you can begin working with your child's problems while he or she is still young. She also points out typical parental behaviors that can destroy a child's self-esteem and suggests alternatives that build instead.

Kay Kuzma, Ed. D., is a child-development specialist and author of over a dozen books on child guidance. She is the speaker on the daily syndicated "Family Matters" radio broadcast and the founder and president of Family Matters, Inc., a nonprofit organization that provides educational materials, seminars, and media presentations designed to improve parenting skills. For a free newsletter, write to Family Matters, P. O. Box 7000 Cleveland, TN 37320

ISBN 0-8163-0833-0

9 780816 308330